Hufnal's Books
2814 N. Hartung Ave.
Milwaukee, WI 53210

Available from:

www.createspace.com

www.amazon.com

ISBN-13: 978-1544862569

ISBN-10: 1544862563

This Book Belongs to……..

This book is dedicated to all children who have a
hunger for learning about nature.
A special thanks to Heidi Lindstadt for technical
support.   You are awesome!

Written and Illustrated by:
Amy Hufnal

The Cooper's Hawk is found in the city and countryside in all parts of the United States. They like to fly through both **deciduous** and coniferous forests as well as meadows. They are a smaller hawk but are voracious eaters, hunting chipmunks, small birds, squirrels and even an occasional chicken. They are powerful fliers and you can see them gliding in the sky. This hawk can fly up to 55 miles per hour and can live for more than 8 years in the wild. The female will lay 3-6 eggs and watch them closely when they hatch, protecting them for the first few weeks of their lives.

Color what the hawk has on his menu.

The Malachite Kingfisher is a petite kingfisher that lives near slow streams and quiet lakes in Kenya, Africa. This bird sits on a branch above the water and watches for small fish to swim by. When the kingfisher sees its prey, he **plunges** into the water very fast to catch the fish. His pointed bill opens and grabs the small fish. Then he heads to the branch again to have his dinner. His feathers are iridescent and seems to change colors depending on how the sunlight bounces off them. These birds are 6 to 7 inches long and they live in the wild for up to 15 years.

Color the small fish that the Malachite Kingfisher eats.

The African Crowned Crane lives on the savannah and can be seen walking slowly through the tall grasses of Kenya and Tanzania, East Africa. They are magnificent birds with pale blue eyes, a wing span of 3.5 feet and are 6 1/2 feet tall. They love to "dance" and display for their mates. They are **omnivores** so they eat insects, worms, frogs, grasses and seeds. They will also attack and eat snakes. The female will lay 2 to 5 eggs per cycle.

Color the different insects that the African Crowned Crane eats.

The Tufted Puffin is an interesting
ocean bird and if you want to see them,
you must take a boat way out into the
Pacific Ocean to large rock islands where
they nest. They have a beautiful black body
with cream feather tufts and an **elegant**
orange beak. They dig a burrow with their
beak and feet, lining it with grasses and feathers.
They lay only 1 egg at a time and it hatches
in about 45 days. They eat fish but may
eat an occasional squid if they can catch one.

Color the squid that the puffin eats.

The Keel-Billed Toucan is found
in the rain forests of Central and
South America. This bird is one of
the most colorful of all the toucans. Its beautiful
bill, although very large, is light weight and does
not make the bird loose its balance when
perching on trees. The equally colorful **plumage**
is black, green, yellow and vibrant read under
the tail. The Keel-Billed toucan is about
17 – 22 inches long. These birds love to eat
fruit and seeds but sometimes will eat lizards.

Color the toucan's next meal.

The Eastern Blue Jay is a pretty
bird that can be found in all of the
states east of the Mississippi.
They are very **vocal** birds, letting others
know they are in the area. Many people
think the blue jay is a pest as they often
steal and eat eggs of other birds. Their
striking black chin strap stands out against
their white throat and their royal blue feathers
look beautiful against the bright sunlit sky.
They live in the forests and are about 9 – 12
inches in length. Their main diet is nuts and
seeds.

Color the nuts and seeds that make up most
of the blue jays diet.

The Brown Pelican is found in many of the world's oceans. They glide over the ocean waves near the shore, using their gigantic wings to propel them just feet above the water. Their long wings allow for very little wind resistance and their long bill expands when they plunge into the water to catch fish. They also eat turtles and <u>crustaceans</u>. Air sacs in their bones help them stay afloat on the water and webbed feet help them move slowly as they bob up and down on the waves.

Color the pelican's dinner – the turtle.

The Hoatzin Bird can only be found in South America living near the Amazon River and its tributaries. It has beautiful blue facial skin, red eyes and a red-brown feathered crest. This bird is very clumsy and spends most of its time near the water on branches. The hoatzin are very rare birds that are strictly **herbivores**. They eat lots of different leaves including succulent plants and spend 4 hours a day munching on these yummy plants. Females lay 2 to 5 eggs and the entire colony helps to raise the baby birds.

Color all the leaves that the Hoatzin enjoys eating.

The Secretary Bird is a magnificent bird and
is found in East Africa. These birds are
quite tall and are usually seen walking through
the tall grass on the **savannah**.
They are light grayish black and many people
think they look like they are wearing black capris
above their long pink, lower legs. Their beak is used
to tear apart reptiles, dangerous snakes and small
mammals after they have kicked and tackled their
prey with their strong feet. The male and female
sleep on the tops of acacia trees where they
build huge nests. Both birds are between4 and
5 feet tall and they have a wing span of 7 feet.

Color the next meal of the Secretary Bird.

The Peacock is the national bird
of India. The male uses his
colorful feathers to display and
attract a mate. These feathers have
iridescent "eye spots" which make him
quite handsome. Peacocks are very good
watch dogs and warn others when a **predator**
is around. These birds like to sit in trees
with few leaves so that they can see far and wide.
Peacocks eat seeds, grasses, fruits and
if they can find one, they will eat a snake.
They lay 3 – 6 eggs per clutch.

Color the snake that the peacock eats.

The Purple Gallinule is sometimes mistaken for a duck but believe it or not, it is not a duck. It has huge feet and long toes that help it to walk on lily pads without sinking. This bird is found in the Southeastern part of the United States where there are ponds with enough **vegetation** to keep them healthy. Gallinules eat a wide variety of seeds but also eat small frogs, snails, water bugs and fish. They lay up to 10 eggs and the eggs are buff colored with brown spots.

Color the Purple Gallinules dinner.

The North American Common Pheasant lives on the ground and is the state bird of South Dakota. It is also known as the Ring-Necked Pheasant because of the white ring around his neck. Pheasants love to clean themselves by taking dust baths. This removes any oils that have built up on their feathers. Pheasants **forage** for their food by digging and pecking the ground. They eat seeds, berries, many small insects and even corn on the cob! (without butter and salt of course)

Color the insects and corn these birds eat.

The Common Loon lives in the northern part of the United States and loves deep freshwater lakes. It has a satiny dark black/green head with beautiful white markings. Their eyes are a deep red and a very sharp, thick bill helps them catch fish. Loon pairs stay together for life and the babies ride on their moms backs until they can swim on their own.

The loon has a very haunting call and sounds like someone is crying. They eat fish, **amphibians** and other prey like crabs. They like to build their nests in shallow parts of a lake using weeds, plant material and cat tail fluff.

Color the Common Loons next meal.

The Burrowing Owl is a very interesting owl. They are found in the western part of the United States, Florida and as far south as South America. These owls live under ground and often times will use an **abandoned** prairie dog or badger den. They have long legs, making them look funny. Their lemon yellow eyes peer out of their burrows in the early morning hoping to spot an insect or lizard. These owls must eat more than their weight every day to survive. The female will lay up to 11 eggs and both birds will take turns sitting on them.

Color the owl's yummy breakfast.

WORD LIST

Abandoned – not lived in
Amphibians – cold-blooded frogs, toads or newts
Bogs – wet, spongy ground
Crustaceans - aquatic animals that have a shell
Deciduous – trees which lose their leaves
Elegant – very beautiful, splendid
Forage – to dig or hunt for food
Herbivore – eating only plant material
Omnivores – eating both meat & veggies
Plumage – the feathers of birds
Plunges – to enter quickly/forcefully
Predator – to hunt for food
Savannah – open land with scattered trees
Vegetation – plant life
Vocal – musical sounds produced by birds